Spotlight on Literacy

AUTHORS

ELAINE MEI AOKI • VIRGINIA ARNOLD • JAMES FLOOD • JAMES V. HOFFMAN • DIANE LAPP

MIRIAM MARTINEZ • ANNEMARIE SULLIVAN PALINCSAR • MICHAEL PRIESTLEY • CARL B. SMITH

WILLIAM H. TEALE • JOSEFINA VILLAMIL TINAJERO • ARNOLD W. WEBB • KAREN D. WOOD

 Macmillan
McGraw-Hill

NEW YORK • FARMINGTON

Unit 1

Take a Closer Look

5

Unit 2

SURPRISES

ALONG THE WAY

7

Hattie
and the
Fox

Written by Mem Fox
Illustrated by Patricia Mullins

12

Hattic was a big black hen.
One morning she looked up and said,
"Goodness gracious me!
I can see a nose in the bushes!"

"Good grief!" said the goose.
"Well, well!" said the pig.

"Who cares?" said the sheep.
"So what?" said the horse.
"What next?" said the cow.

And Hattie said,
"Goodness gracious me!
I can see a nose
and two eyes in the bushes!"

"Good grief!" said the goose.
"Well, well!" said the pig.
"Who cares?" said the sheep.
"So what?" said the horse.
"What next?" said the cow.

And Hattie said,
"Goodness gracious me!
I can see a nose, two eyes,
and two ears in the bushes!"

"Good grief!" said the goose.
"Well, well!" said the pig.
"Who cares?" said the sheep.
"So what?" said the horse.
"What next?" said the cow.

And Hattie said,
"Goodness gracious me!
I can see a nose, two eyes, two ears,
and two legs in the bushes!"

"Good grief!" said the goose.
"Well, well!" said the pig.
"Who cares?" said the sheep.
"So what?" said the horse.
"What next?" said the cow.

And Hattie said,
"Goodness gracious me!
I can see a nose, two eyes, two ears, two legs,
and a body in the bushes!"

"Good grief!" said the goose.
"Well, well!" said the pig.
"Who cares?" said the sheep.
"So what?" said the horse.
"What next?" said the cow.

And Hattie said,
"Goodness gracious me!
I can see a nose, two eyes, two ears, a body, four legs,
and a tail in the bushes!
It's a fox! It's a fox!"
And she flew very quickly into a nearby tree.

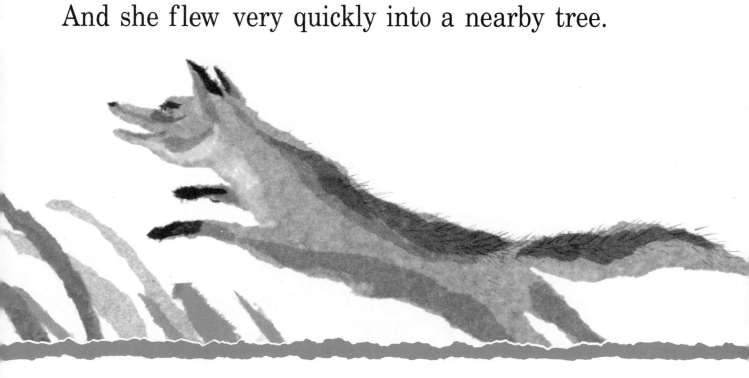

"Oh, no!" said the goose.
"Dear me!" said the pig.
"Oh, dear!" said the sheep.
"Oh, help!" said the horse.

But the cow said, "MOO!"

so loudly that the fox was frightened and ran away.

And they were all so surprised
that none of them said anything
for a very long time.

41

Meet Mem Fox

When Mem Fox visits schools, she often invites children to read *Hattie and the Fox* aloud with her. She says it's lots of fun to say the words fast and then to say what the cow says in a very slow, deep voice.

Ms. Fox likes this story for other reasons, too. "There are many old stories about hens and foxes," she says. "But this one is new."

Mem Fox loves to read and write. She says, "Reading is the best way to learn how to write. Reading written words and hearing written words have taught me to write well."

Meet Patricia Mullins

To make the pictures for *Hattie and the Fox,* Patricia Mullins visited a special farm in the middle of a city. She went there every day to look at the animals and make drawings of them. "I always start my pictures by drawing live animals," she says. "I watch how they move. That helps me make them look more real in my pictures."

Later, Ms. Mullins tore pieces of colored tissue paper to look like the animals. Then she glued them down. Last, she used a crayon to draw a few lines. This way of making pictures is called collage.

OPEN

I open my eyes.

I open the curtains.

I open my mouth to say "good morning."

At breakfast time

I open the refrigerator.

"I'm going out" I say,

and open the door.

Like opening a new book,

one day starts.

Chikaoka Saori, fourth grade

45

ANY KIND OF DOG

by Lynn Reiser

Richard wanted a dog, any kind of dog.

But his mother said
a dog was
too much trouble,

so she gave him a caterpillar.

The caterpillar was very nice.
It looked a little like a dog,

Lhasa Apso

but it was not a dog.
Richard wanted a dog.
His mother said
a dog was too much trouble,

so she gave him a mouse.

The mouse was very nice.
It looked a little like a dog,

Chihuahua

but it was not a dog.
Richard wanted a dog.
His mother said
a dog was too much trouble,

so she gave him a baby alligator.

The baby alligator was very nice.
It looked a little like a dog,

Dachshund

but it was not a dog.
Richard wanted a dog.
His mother said
a dog was too much trouble,

so she gave him a lamb.

The lamb was very nice.
It looked a little like a dog,

Bedlington
Terrier

but it was not a dog.
Richard wanted a dog.
His mother said
a dog was too much trouble,

so she gave him a pony.

The pony was very nice.
It looked a little like a dog,

Great Dane

but it was not a dog.
Richard wanted a dog.
His mother said
a dog was too much trouble,

so she gave him a lion.

The lion was very nice.
It looked a little like a dog,

Chow Chow

but it was not a dog.
Richard wanted a dog.
His mother said
a dog was too much trouble,

so she gave him a bear.

The bear was very nice.
It looked a little like a dog,

Newfoundland

but it was not a dog.

All of the animals were very nice,

but Richard still wanted a dog.

So his mother gave him a dog.

The dog was very nice.

It looked exactly like a dog.

Just a Dog

The dog was a lot of trouble,

but
it was
worth it.

Meet
LYNN REISER

Lynn Reiser is a doctor. She has always loved
to read and draw. A few years ago, someone
asked her to draw the pictures for a book of
songs. She had a great time doing them!
Now she writes and draws her own books.
Ms. Reiser wrote *Any Kind of Dog* when her
family wanted to get a dog. She says, "I like
writing because it can be shared with other
people. I want children to enjoy reading as
much as I do."

A "Wild" Alphabet

Do you see the alphabet letters in these pictures? They are really markings on the wings of butterflies.

This butterfly has letters on its wings too. Which ones do you see?

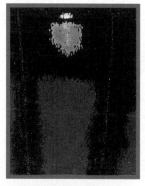

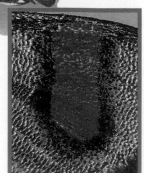

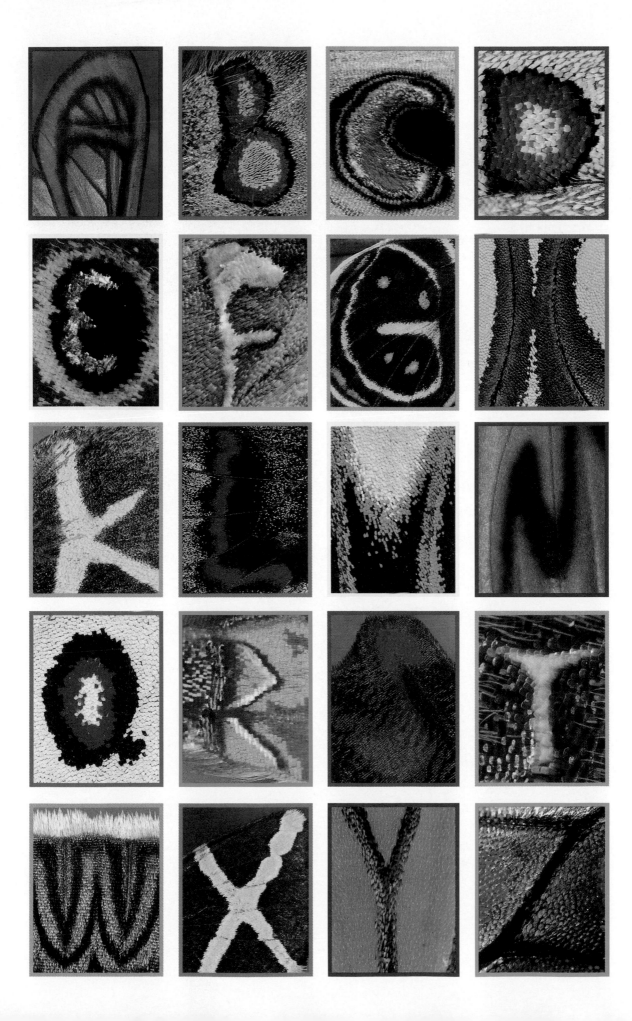

La NUBE

Nube-conejo,

nube-alacrăn,

nube-velero,

nube-volcăn,

nube-tinaja,

nube-cabeza,

nube-elefante,

nube-caleza.

Si un solo instante
miro a otro lado,
cuando me vuelvo
tŭ ya has cambiado.

Emma Pérez

The CLOUD

Cloud-rabbit,

cloud-scorpion,

cloud-sailboat,

cloud-volcano,

cloud-pitcher,

cloud-head,

cloud-elephant,

cloud-carriage.

If for a moment

I glance away,

and then turn back,

you've changed again.

Emma Pérez

73

Seven Sillies

Written by Joyce Dunbar
Illustrated by Chris Downing

On a bright and shining morning,
Pig looked into the pond.

"There's a pig in the pond," said Pig.
"Such a handsome pig!"

And Pig called over to Sheep.

"What do you see in the pond?" asked Pig.
"I see a pig and a sheep," answered Sheep.
"Such a beautiful sheep!"

And Sheep called over to Goat.

"What do you see in the pond?" asked Sheep.
"I see a pig and a sheep and a goat,"
answered Goat.
"Such a gorgeous goat."

And Goat called over to Rabbit.

"What do you see in the pond?" asked Goat.
"I see a pig and a sheep and a goat
and a rabbit," answered Rabbit.
"Such a splendid rabbit!"

And Rabbit called over to Hen.

"What do you see in the pond?"
asked Rabbit.

"I see a pig and a sheep and a goat and
a rabbit and a hen," said Hen.

"Such a fine, feathered hen."

And Hen called over to Mouse.

"What do you see in the pond?" asked Hen. "I see a pig and a sheep and a goat and a rabbit and a hen and a mouse," said Mouse. "Such a dear, little mouse."

And Mouse called over to Frog.

"What do you see in the pond?"
asked Mouse.

"I see seven sillies," answered Frog.

"Seven sillies?" asked the pig and the sheep and the goat and the rabbit and the hen and the mouse. "What do you mean?"

"They are all in the pond and they want to get out," said Frog.

"How can we get them out?"

"You will have to jump in and fetch them,"
answered Frog.

So the pig and the sheep and the goat and
the rabbit and the hen and the mouse all
jumped into the water with a *splash!*

"There is nothing in the pond, after all!"
they said.

"Oh, yes, there is," laughed Frog.
"There is a handsome pig,
a beautiful sheep,
a gorgeous goat,

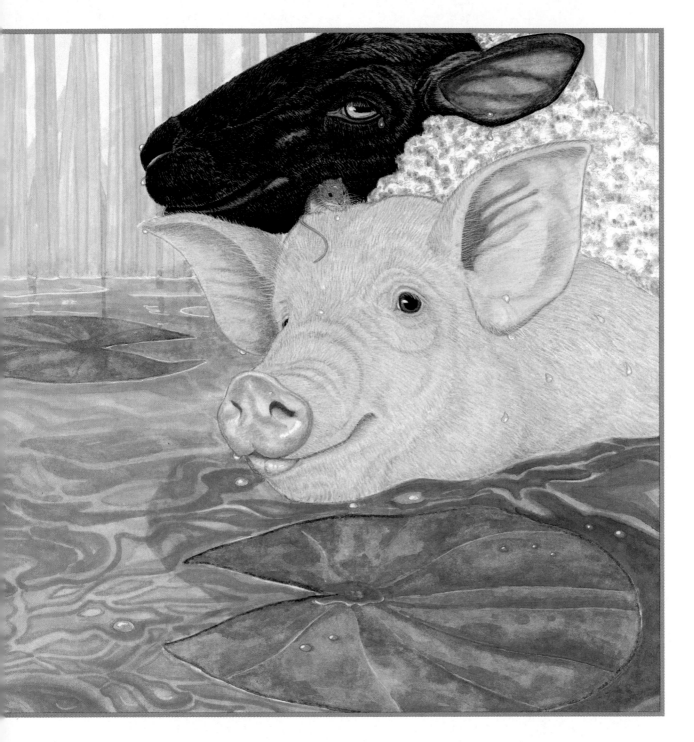

a splendid rabbit,
a fine, feathered hen,
a dear, little mouse,
and that makes seven sillies."

The animals scrambled out of the pond all
sopping and dripping with water. They did
feel very silly!

Then . . .

"How many sillies?" asked Pig.

"Seven," said Frog.

Pig began to count.

The other animals joined in.

"One, two, three, four, five, six—"
The only one left was Frog.
"Aha!" they laughed. "SEVEN SILLIES!"

"We see a frog that can't count," they said.

"Such a silly frog!"

MEET

Joyce Dunbar

Joyce Dunbar was an English teacher for many years. Then she became deaf and stopped teaching. Ms. Dunbar has always liked to write. Now she has more time to work on her writing. Her family gave her the idea to write for children. She says, "I like to write in the mornings. Then I like to spend the afternoons gardening." Even when she is not writing, she thinks about it all the time. Ms. Dunbar says she even thinks about writing in her sleep!

MEET
Chris Downing

Chris Downing loves to draw and paint animals. He was happy when Joyce Dunbar asked him to illustrate *Seven Sillies*. "I am very proud of *Seven Sillies*. I hope that all children will enjoy it," he says. Chris Downing used photographs so his animals would seem real.

Mr. Downing lives in England with his wife and two small children. Sometimes he uses his family as models for his art. Chris Downing hopes to illustrate many more children's books.

First Snow

Snow makes whiteness where it falls.
The bushes look like popcorn-balls.
And places where I always play,
Look like somewhere else today.

Marie Louise Allen

Meet JAN ORMEROD

Jan Ormerod was a child in Australia when she first heard *The Story of Chicken Licken*. "In some other countries, Chicken Licken is called Chicken Little," she says.

She thought it would be fun to have this book tell two stories. "The words tell about Chicken Licken," she says. "The pictures tell another story."

At the time Ms. Ormerod wrote this story, she had a baby that crawled everywhere. "I know the trouble a crawling baby can get into," she says.

Since Ms. Ormerod wrote this book, many school-children have invited her to see their own plays and puppet shows using the Chicken Licken story.

by
Jan
Ormerod

THE STORY OF
CHICKEN
LICKEN

OH, DUCK LUCK, DON'T GO!
I was going and I met Henny Penny,
and Henny Penny met Chicken Licken
and the sky had fallen
on her poor little head.
Now we are going to tell the king.

OH, DRAKE LAKE, DON'T GO!
I was going and I met Cock Lock,
and Cock Lock met Henny Penny,
and Henny Penny met Chicken Licken
and the sky had fallen
    on her poor little head.
        Now we are going to tell the king.

OH, GOOSE LOOSE, DON'T GO!
I was going and I met Duck Luck,
and Duck Luck met Cock Lock,
and Cock Lock met Henny Penny,
and Henny Penny met Chicken Licken
and the sky had fallen
on her poor little head.
Now we are going to tell the king.

OH, GANDER LANDER, DON'T GO!
I was going and I met Drake Lake,
and Drake Lake met Duck Luck,
and Duck Luck met Cock Lock,
and Cock Lock met Henny Penny,
and Henny Penny met Chicken Licken
and the sky had fallen
on her poor little head.
Now we are going to tell the king.

So Gander Lander turned back and met Turkey Lurkey. He asked Turkey Lurkey where he was going.

I am going to the woods for some food.

OH, TURKEY LURKEY, DON'T GO!
I was going and I met Goose Loose,
and Goose Loose met Drake Lake,
and Drake Lake met Duck Luck,
and Duck Luck met Cock Lock,
and Cock Lock met Henny Penny,
and Henny Penny met
Chicken Licken and the sky
had fallen on her poor little head.
Now we are going to tell the king.

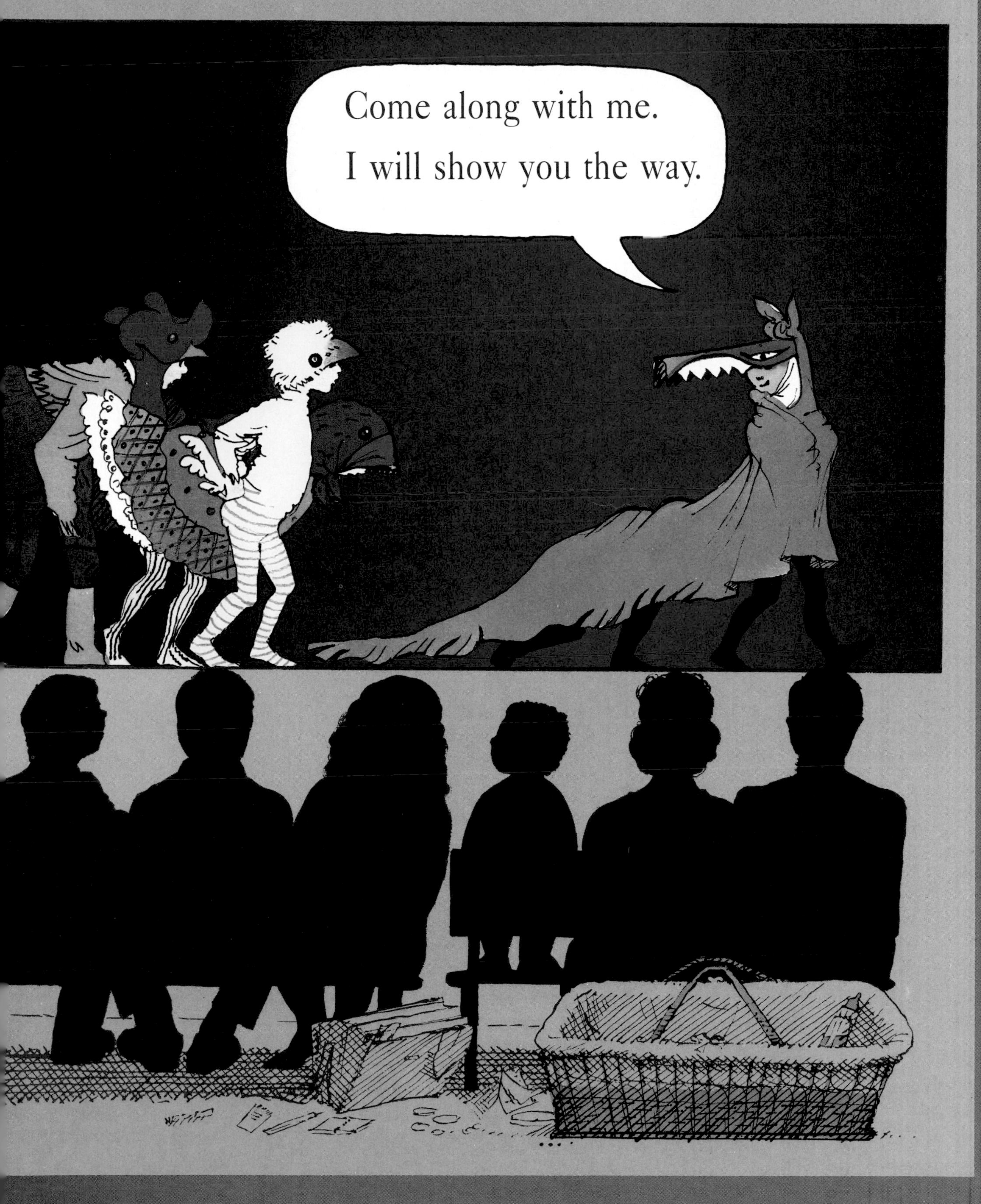
Come along with me.
I will show you the way.

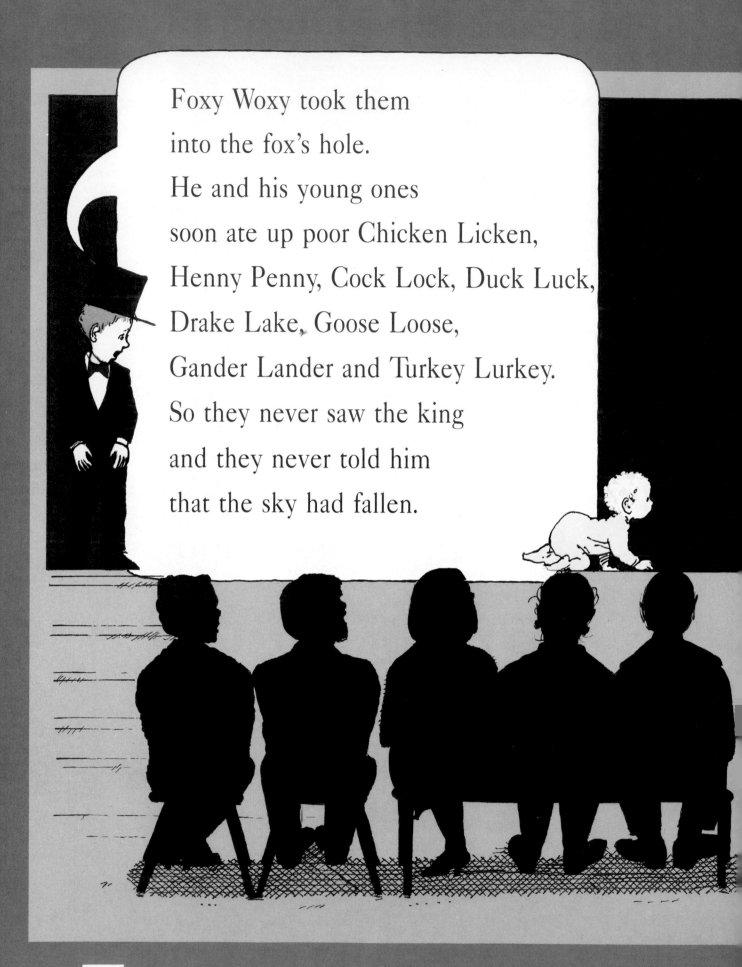

Foxy Woxy took them
into the fox's hole.
He and his young ones
soon ate up poor Chicken Licken,
Henny Penny, Cock Lock, Duck Luck,
Drake Lake, Goose Loose,
Gander Lander and Turkey Lurkey.
So they never saw the king
and they never told him
that the sky had fallen.

Magic in Mother

A Story Without Words by Sally Lucas

Gooseland

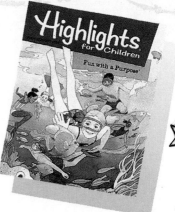

Illustrated by Liisa Chauncy Guida

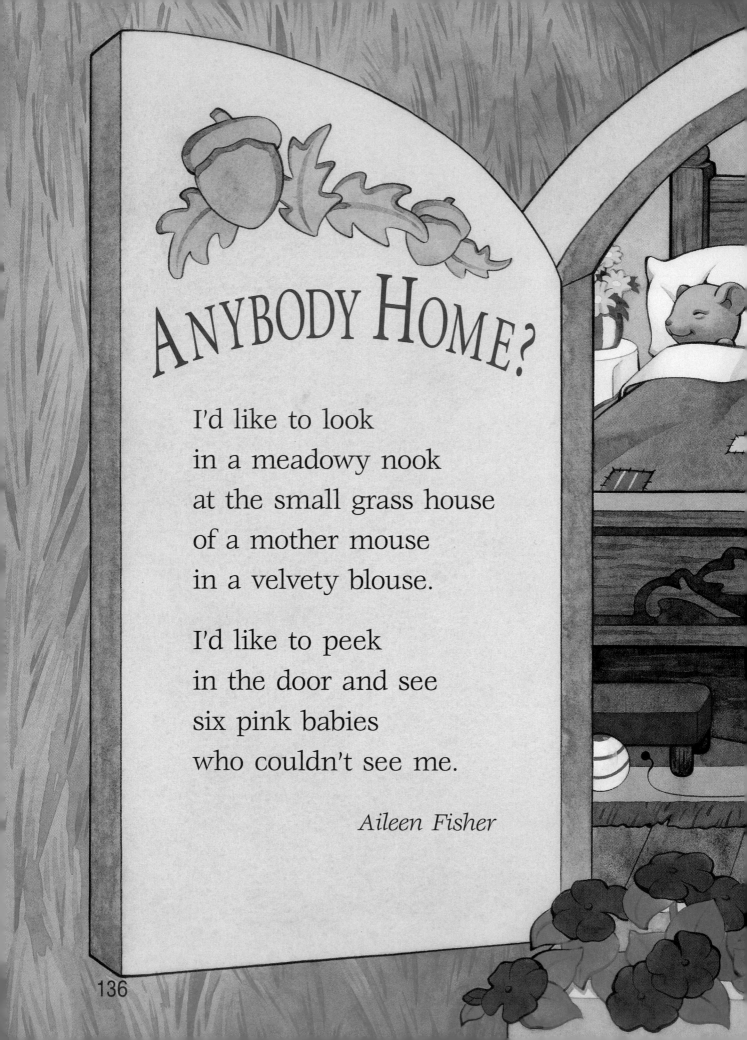

ANYBODY HOME?

I'd like to look
in a meadowy nook
at the small grass house
of a mother mouse
in a velvety blouse.

I'd like to peek
in the door and see
six pink babies
who couldn't see me.

Aileen Fisher

ONE MONDAY MORNING

Text and pictures by Uri Shulevitz

142

One Monday morning

143

the king,

the queen, and the little prince came to visit me.

But I wasn't home.

So the little prince said,
"In that case we shall return on Tuesday."

On Tuesday morning the king, the queen, the
little prince,

and the knight came to visit me.

But I wasn't home.

So the little prince said,

"In that case we shall return on Wednesday."

154

On Wednesday morning
the king,
the queen,
the little prince,
the knight,
and a royal guard
came to visit me.

155

But I wasn't home.

So the little prince said,
"In that case we shall return on Thursday."

On Thursday morning
the king, the queen,
the little prince,
the knight, a royal guard,
and the royal cook
came to visit me.

But I wasn't home.

So the little prince said,

"In that case we shall return on Friday."

On Friday morning
the king, the queen,
the little prince,
the knight, the royal guard,
the royal cook,
and the royal barber
came to visit me.

But I wasn't home.

So the little prince said,

"In that case we shall return on Saturday."

On Saturday morning
the king, the queen,
the little prince,
the knight, a royal guard,
the royal cook,
the royal barber,
and the royal jester
came to visit me.

167

But I wasn't home.

So the little prince said,

"In that case we shall return on Sunday."

On Sunday morning the king, the queen,
the little prince, the knight,
a royal guard,

172

the royal cook,
the royal barber,
the royal jester,
and a little dog
came to visit me.

173

And I was home.

So the little prince said,

"We just dropped in to say hello."

MEET
Uri Shulevitz

Uri Shulevitz was born in Poland.
As a boy he lived in France.
While there, he learned a French
song about a little boy who is visited
by the king. It begins with the words
"One Monday morning the Emperor, his
wife, and his son the little prince came to
visit me . . ." Mr. Shulevitz liked the song
so much he decided to write a story about
it. That story became *One Monday Morning*.

THE FOLK WHO LIVE IN BACKWARD TOWN

The folk who live in Backward Town
Are inside out and upside down.
They wear their hats inside their heads
And go to sleep beneath their beds.
They only eat the apple peeling
And take their walks across the ceiling.

Mary Ann Hoberman

You'll Soon Grow into Them, Titch by Pat Hutchins

Titch needed new pants.

His brother Pete said,
"You can have my old pants,
they're too small for me."

"They're still a bit big for me,"
said Titch.

"You'll soon grow into them,"
said Pete.

And when Titch needed a new sweater,

his sister Mary said,
"You can have my old sweater,
it's too small for me."

"It's still a bit big for me,"
said Titch.

"You'll soon grow into it," said Mary.

And when Titch needed new socks,

they both said,
"You can have our old socks,
they're too small for us."

"And I'll soon grow into them," said Titch.

"I think," said Mother, "that Titch should have some new clothes."

So Dad and Titch went shopping.

They bought a brand-new pair of pants,

a brand-new sweater,

and a brand-new pair of socks.

And when Mother brought
their brand-new baby home,
Titch wore the new clothes.

"There," said Titch,

"he can have my old pants,

201

and my old sweater,

and my old socks.
They're much too small for me!"

"They're a bit big for him,"
said Pete and Mary.

"He'll soon grow into them,"
said Titch.

Meet
Pat Hutchins

Pat Hutchins says, "I wrote *You'll Soon Grow into Them, Titch* for my son Sam. He has an older brother, Morgan. When Morgan grew out of his clothes, he gave them to Sam. Suddenly, we realized that Sam never had any new clothes of his own. So we went out and bought him his own new set of clothes."

About the pictures, Ms. Hutchins tells children, "The story is all about growing, so I put a bird's nest in the pictures. When Mother's baby is born, the baby birds have hatched."

FAMILY CIRCUS

Something  Has Been Here

Something big has been here,
what it was, I do not know,
for I did not see it coming,
and I did not see it go,
but I hope I never meet it,
if I do, I'm in a fix,
for it left behind its footprints,
they are size nine-fifty-six.

Jack Prelutsky

MEET ED YOUNG

Ed Young was born in China in 1931. While he was growing up, China was at war. So his family had to move around a lot. Wherever he went he drew pictures. He also made up plays. Mr. Young always wanted to be an artist. When he was a young man, he moved to the United States. He did a lot of drawing for his job. His friends liked his drawings very much. They thought it would be great for him to draw children's books. So did he.

Today Ed Young has written and drawn more than forty books. He still loves to draw and make up stories. "I have never lost the child in me," he says.

Seven Blind Mice

BY ED YOUNG

One day seven blind mice were surprised
to find a strange Something by their pond.
"What is it?" they cried, and they all ran home.

On Monday, Red Mouse went first to find out.

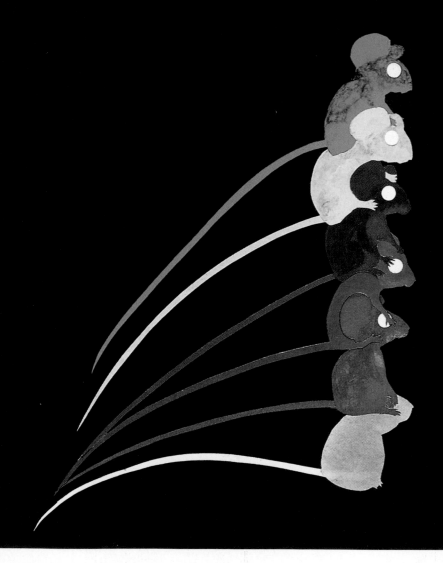

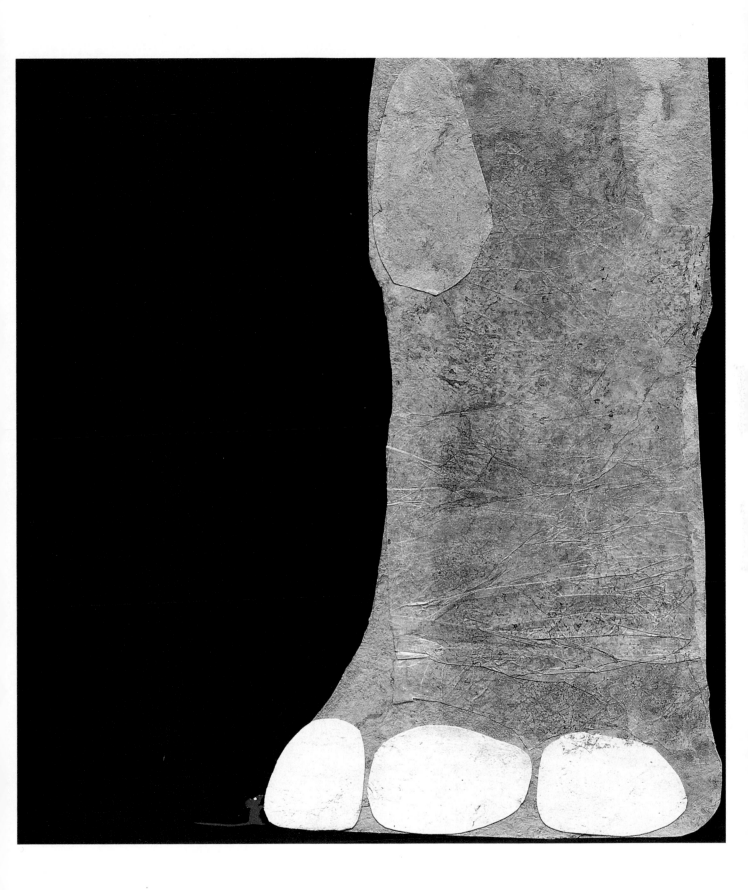

"It's a pillar," he said.
No one believed him.

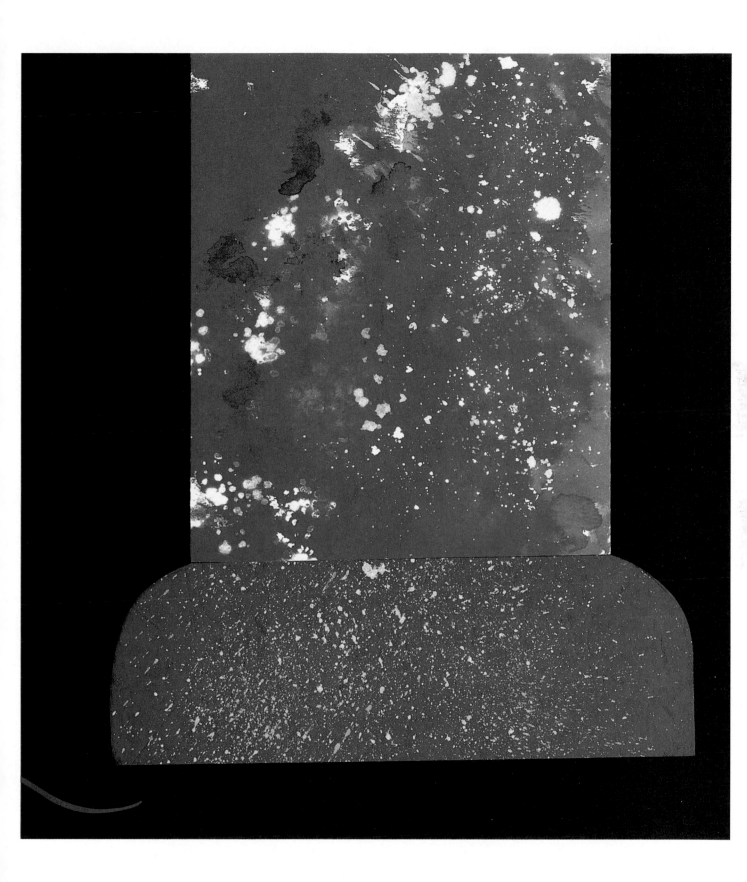

On Tuesday, Green Mouse set out.
He was the second to go.

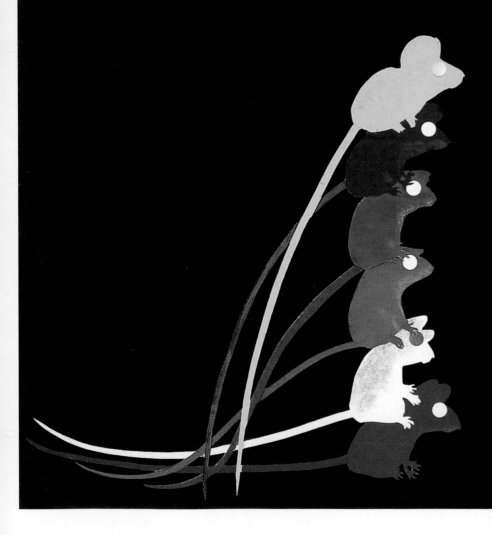

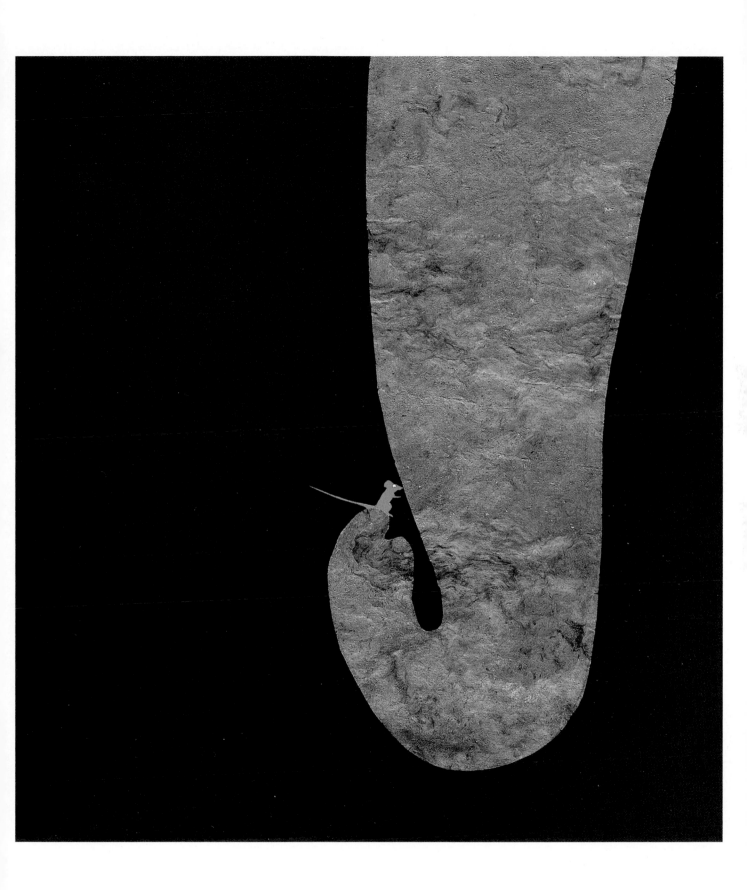

"It's a snake," he said.

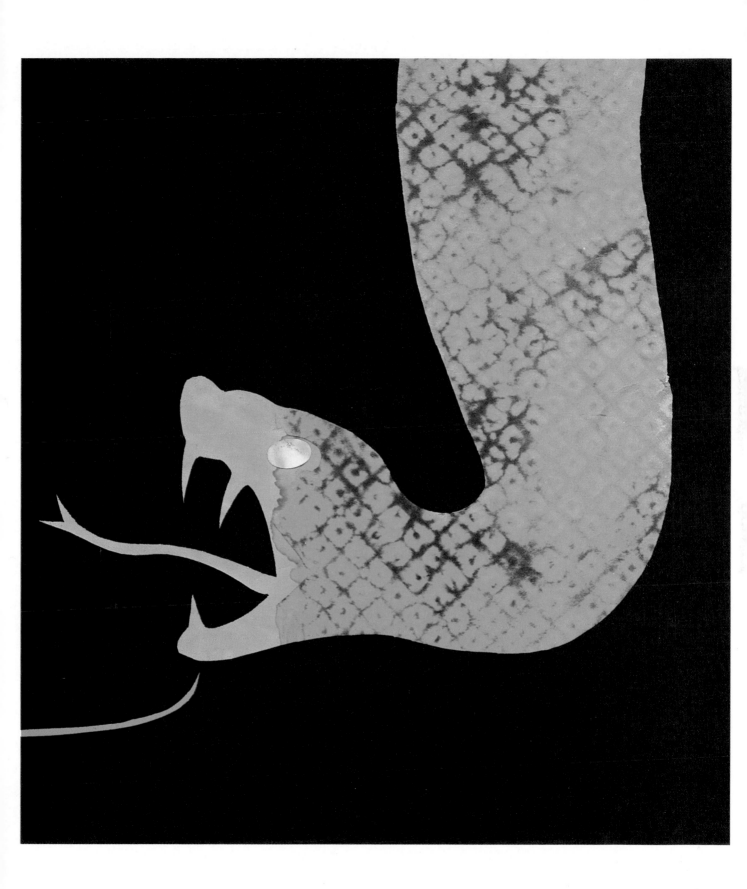

"No," said Yellow Mouse on Wednesday.

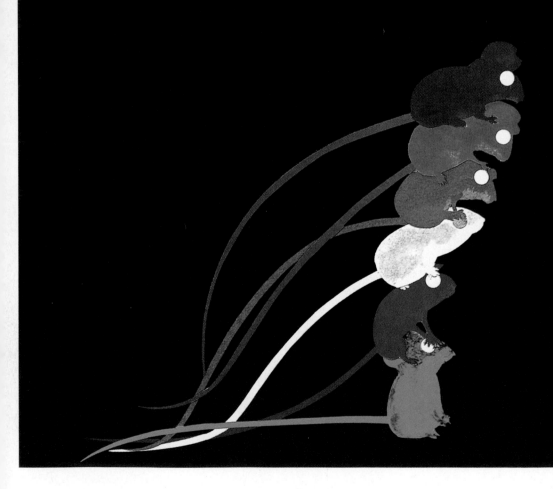

"It's a spear."

He was the third in turn.

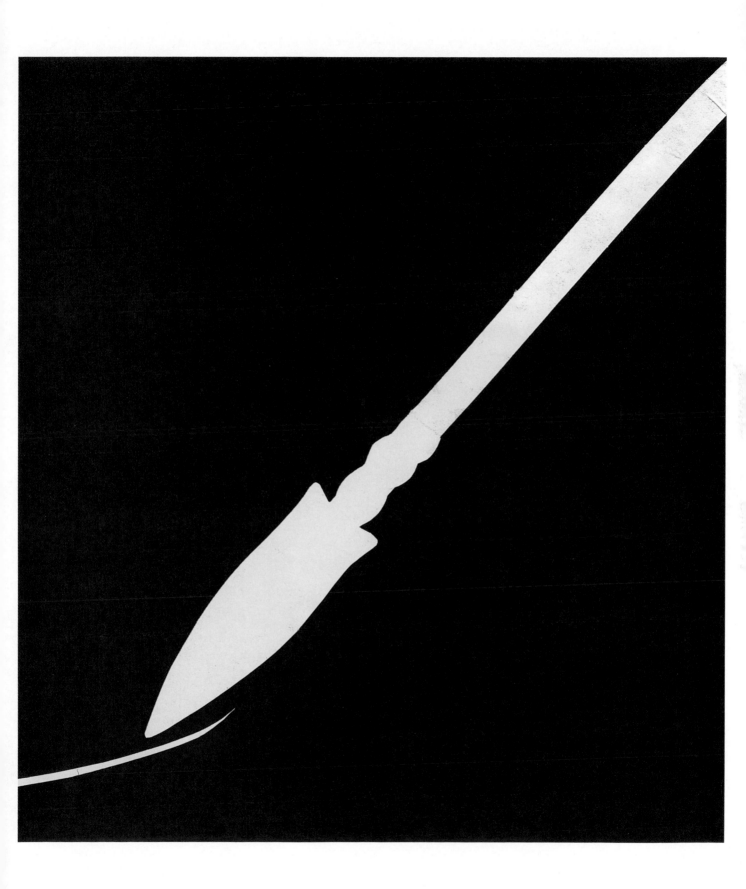

The fourth was Purple Mouse.
He went on Thursday.

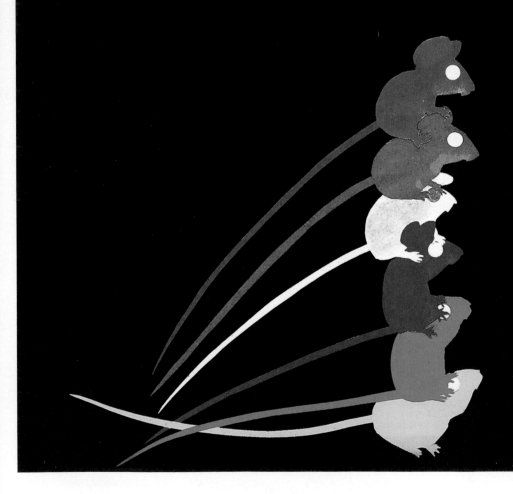

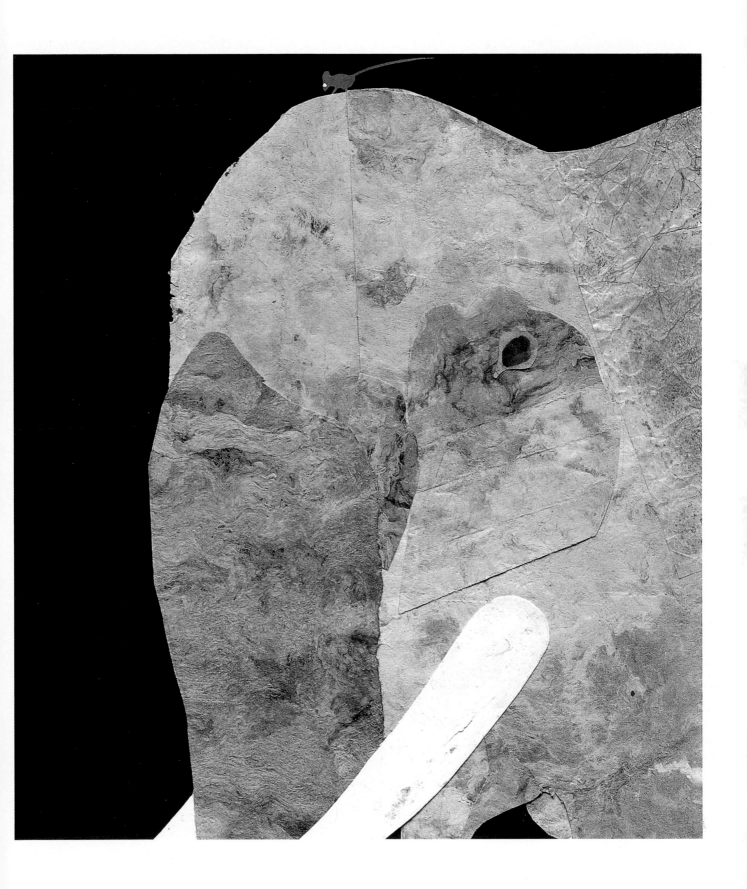

"It's a great cliff," he said.

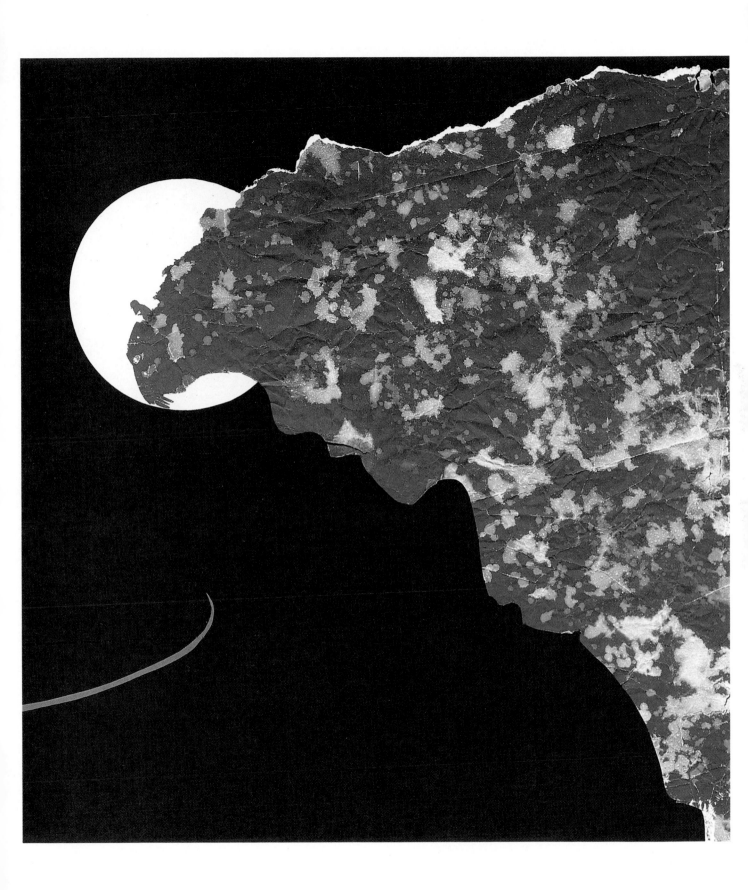

Orange Mouse went on Friday, the fifth to go.

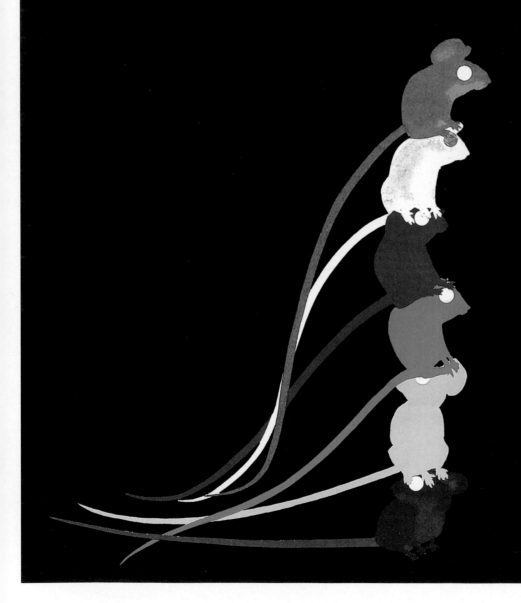

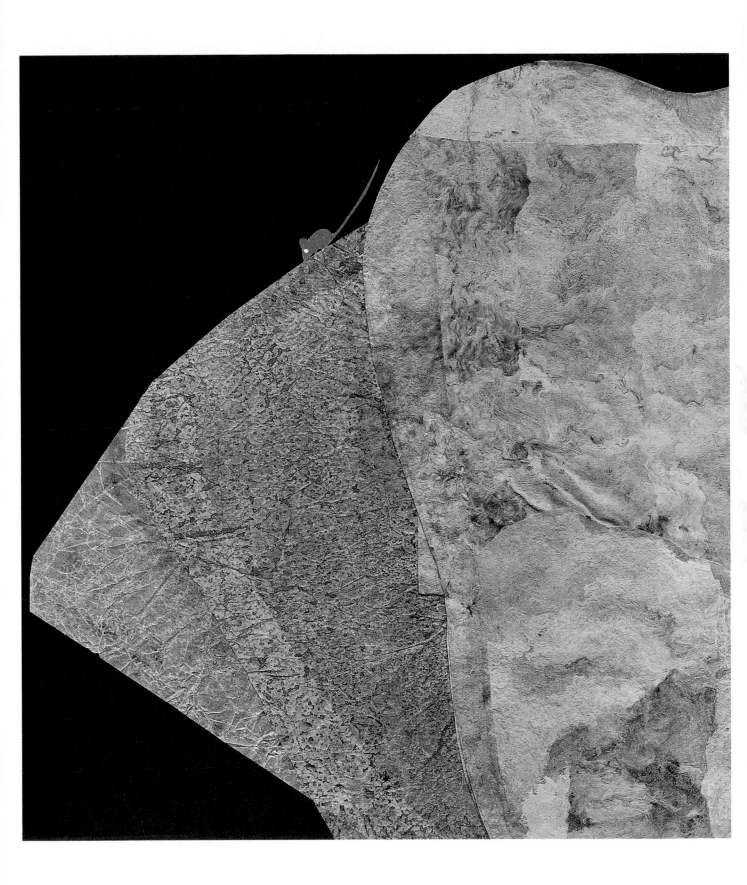

233

"It's a fan!" he cried. "I felt it move."

235

The sixth to go was Blue Mouse.

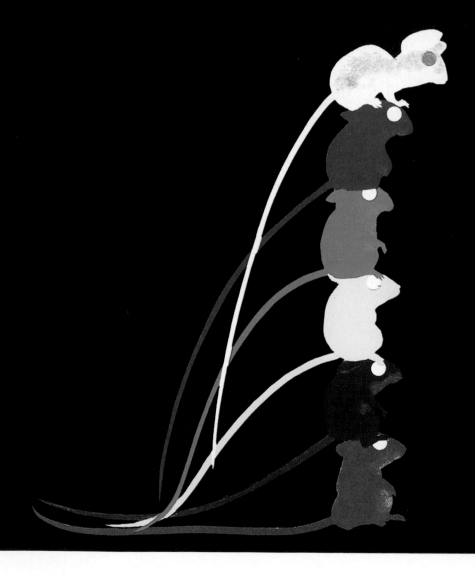

He went on Saturday and said,
"It's nothing but a rope."

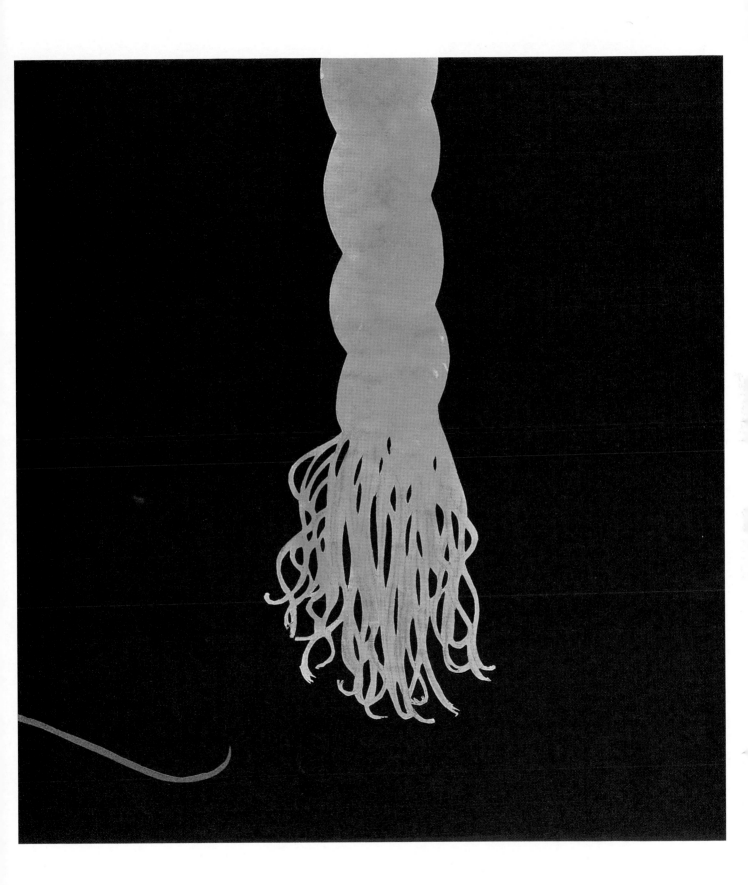

But the others didn't agree.

They began to argue.

"A snake!" "A rope!" "A fan!" "A cliff!"

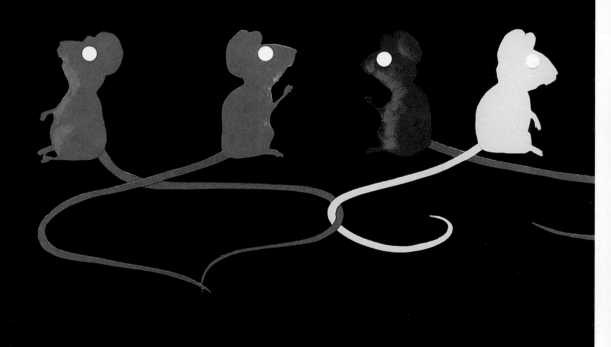

Until on Sunday, White Mouse,
the seventh mouse,
went to the pond.

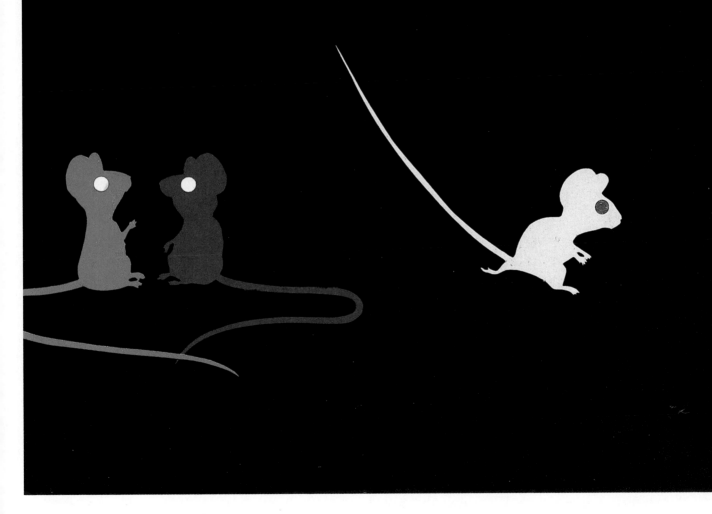

When she came upon the Something, she ran up one side, and she ran down the other. She ran across the top and from end to end.

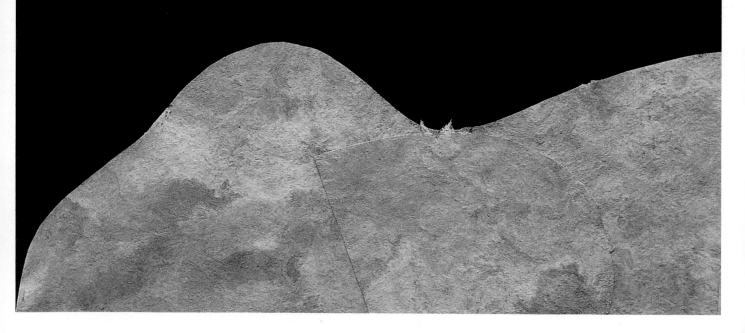

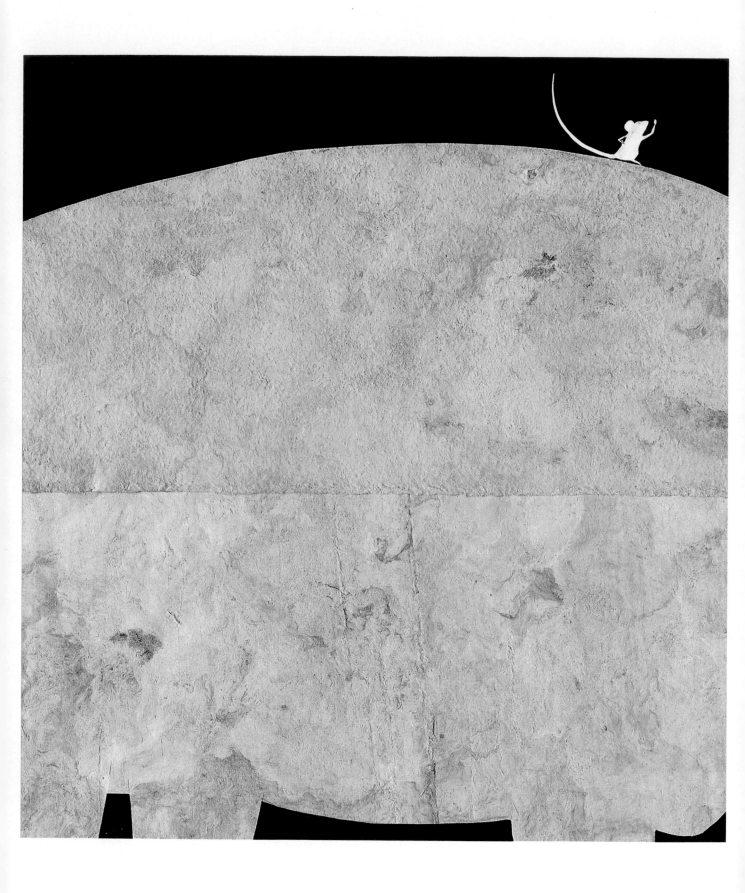

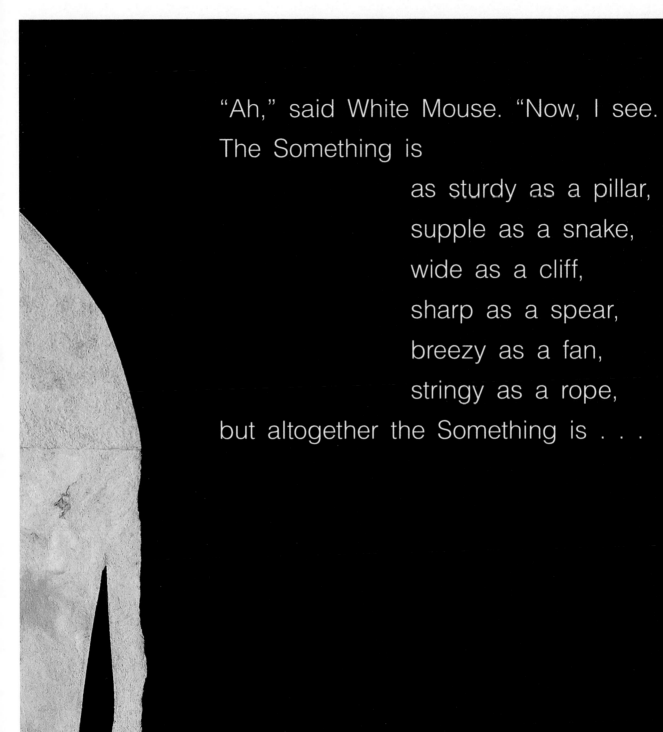

"Ah," said White Mouse. "Now, I see.
The Something is

        as sturdy as a pillar,

        supple as a snake,

        wide as a cliff,

        sharp as a spear,

        breezy as a fan,

        stringy as a rope,

but altogether the Something is . . .

an elephant!"

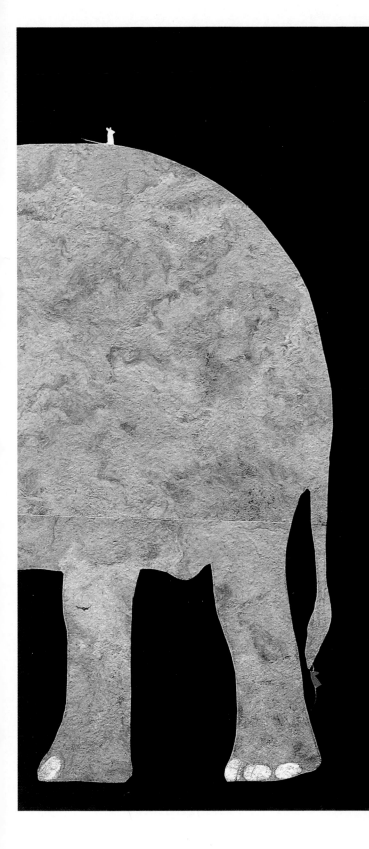

And when the other
mice ran up one side
and down the other,
across the Something
from end to end,
they agreed.
Now they saw, too.

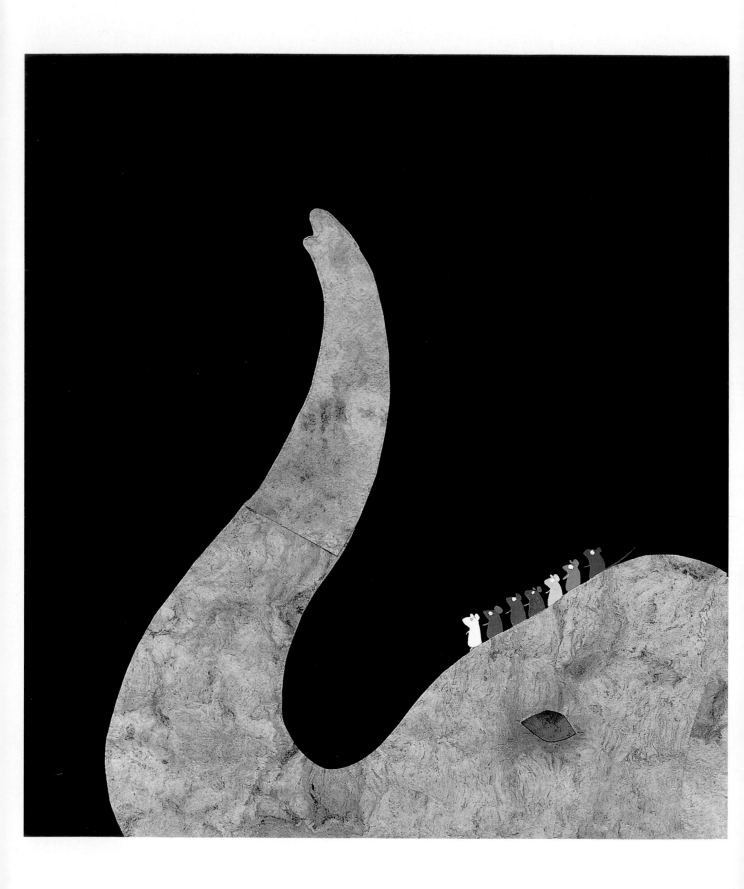

The Mouse Moral:

Knowing in part may make a fine tale,

but wisdom comes from seeing the whole.

THE ELEPHANT'S TRUNK

Your Big Backyard

The elephant's trunk is wonderful. It can do many things.

A mother elephant gently pushes her calf with her trunk. She lets her calf know she is close behind.

An elephant gets
food with its trunk.
It uses the trunk to
pull up grass and
lift it to the mouth.

When an elephant
sleeps, it rests its
trunk. It can fold the
trunk on its tusks.

Elephants use their trunks to play.
They tug and push.
They hold on to each other.

THINGS THAT HAPPEN

Only a while ago,
I saw a snail
running
down the road,
a worm
hopping,
and heard
a toad
singing
like a bird.

The sun rises!
The sun rises!
Can there be
Still more surprises?

Felice Holman

THE SURPRISE FAMILY

by LYNN REISER

First there was an egg.

One day it cracked open.

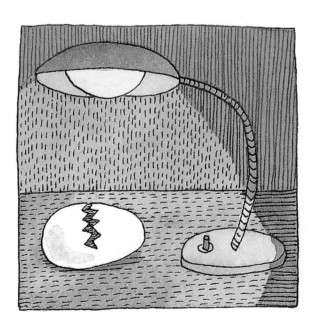

A baby chick looked out.
Nobody was there.

Where was her mother?

The baby chick looked up and saw—

a boy.

Her mother was a boy!
The boy was not the kind of mother
the chick had expected,
but she loved him anyway.

She followed him everywhere.
The boy showed
his baby chick
how to find
water and food
and grit
for her gizzard.

He taught her how to hide
safe inside his jacket
when a hawk flew by
or when the vacuum cleaner
came too close.

Every afternoon
the boy
and his baby chick
went for a walk
around the garden.

At night
she slept warm
under the edge
of his quilt.

The baby chick grew and grew
and became a little hen.

She still followed the boy everywhere,
but now following the boy was not enough.
She wanted a family to follow her.

She built a nest.

The boy found a clutch of eggs.

He gave them to the little hen.

She sat
and warmed the eggs,
and every day she turned the eggs,

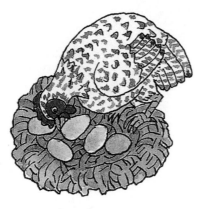

and she sat

and she sat

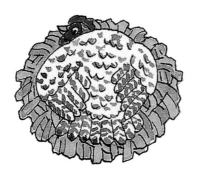

and she sat

and she sat

and she sat—

CRACK!

The eggs cracked open.

The babies looked out
and saw the little hen.

They followed her everywhere.
She showed them how to find
water and food

and grit
for their gizzards.

She taught them to run to her
when she sang a danger song
and danced a danger dance

and to hide
safe under her feathers.

Every afternoon the boy
and the little hen and the babies
went for a walk around the garden.

At night the babies slept

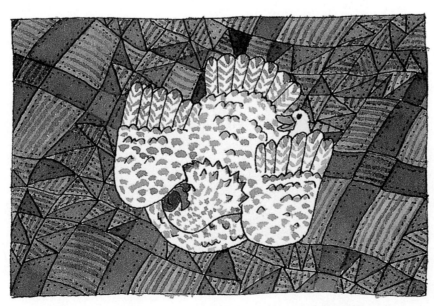

warm under the little hen's wings.

The little hen's family grew.
They still followed her everywhere,
but now walking around the garden
was not enough.
They wanted to walk by the pond.

So the boy
and the hen
took them to walk
by the pond.

They stood at the edge of the water.

They looked at the water.

They took a drink of the water.

They jumped into the water!

The little hen cried her DANGER cry—
her babies splashed.

The little hen danced her DANGER dance—
her babies swam.
The little hen held out her wings
for her babies to run under—

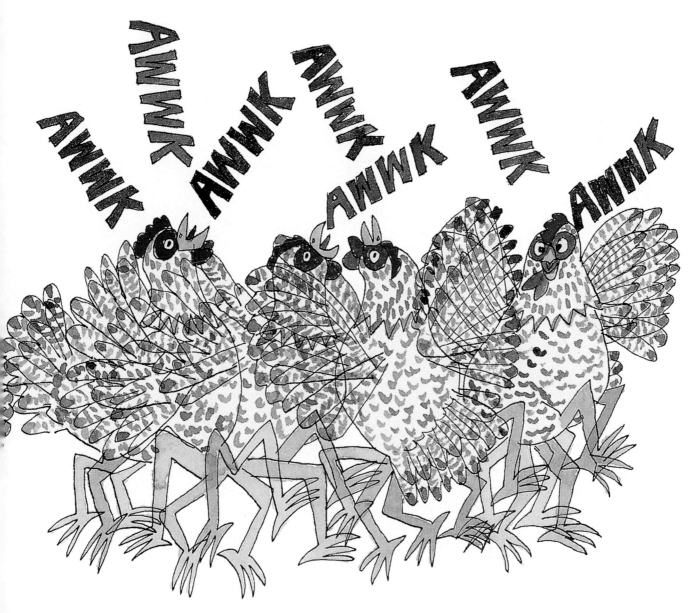

but they kept on swimming
farther and farther away.

The little hen ran after them,
but when her feet got wet,
she stopped.
She was a chicken.
Chickens cannot swim.

The little hen's babies
swam out of sight.

Only her boy was left.

Then the little hen's babies
turned around,

swam back,

hopped out of the water,

flapped their wings,

shook their tails,

and ran to their mother hen.

She gathered her babies in,
warm under her wings.
She looked at them.
They were safe.

She looked at them
again.
Carefully.

Their beaks were not pointed
like her beak,
or soft
like her boy's mouth—
they were flat.

Their feet were not sharp
like her feet,
or hard
like her boy's shoes—
they were webbed.

Their feathers were not fluffy
like her feathers,
or fuzzy
like her boy's jacket—
they were waterproof.

Her babies did not look like chicks
or like boys.
They looked like ducklings.

Ducklings were not the kind of family
she had expected,

but she loved them anyway.

The ducklings grew
and grew and became
big ducks.
Some afternoons
while the ducks
swam in the pond,
the boy
walked around the garden,
and the hen followed him.
Some afternoons
while the ducks
swam in the pond,
the hen
walked around the garden,
and the boy followed her.
Other afternoons
while the ducks
swam in the pond,
and the boy waded after
them, the hen watched.

But every afternoon
in the garden
beside the pond,
after walking and swimming and wading,
there they all were,
together,
under the little hen's wings.

QUACK

MEET LYNN REISER

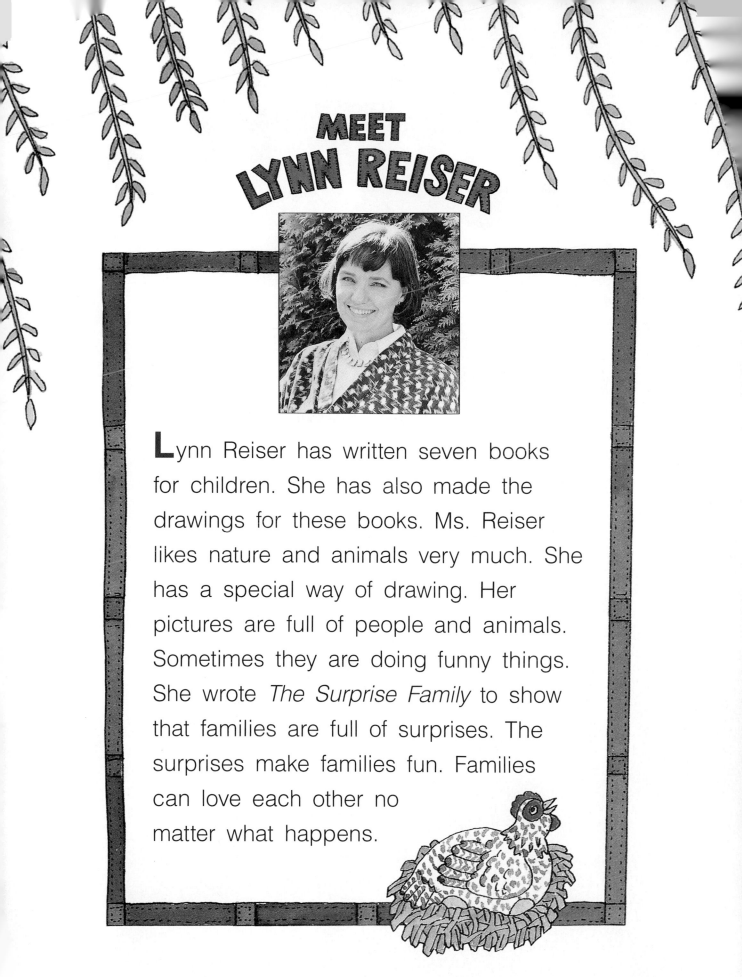

Lynn Reiser has written seven books for children. She has also made the drawings for these books. Ms. Reiser likes nature and animals very much. She has a special way of drawing. Her pictures are full of people and animals. Sometimes they are doing funny things. She wrote *The Surprise Family* to show that families are full of surprises. The surprises make families fun. Families can love each other no matter what happens.

Surprises

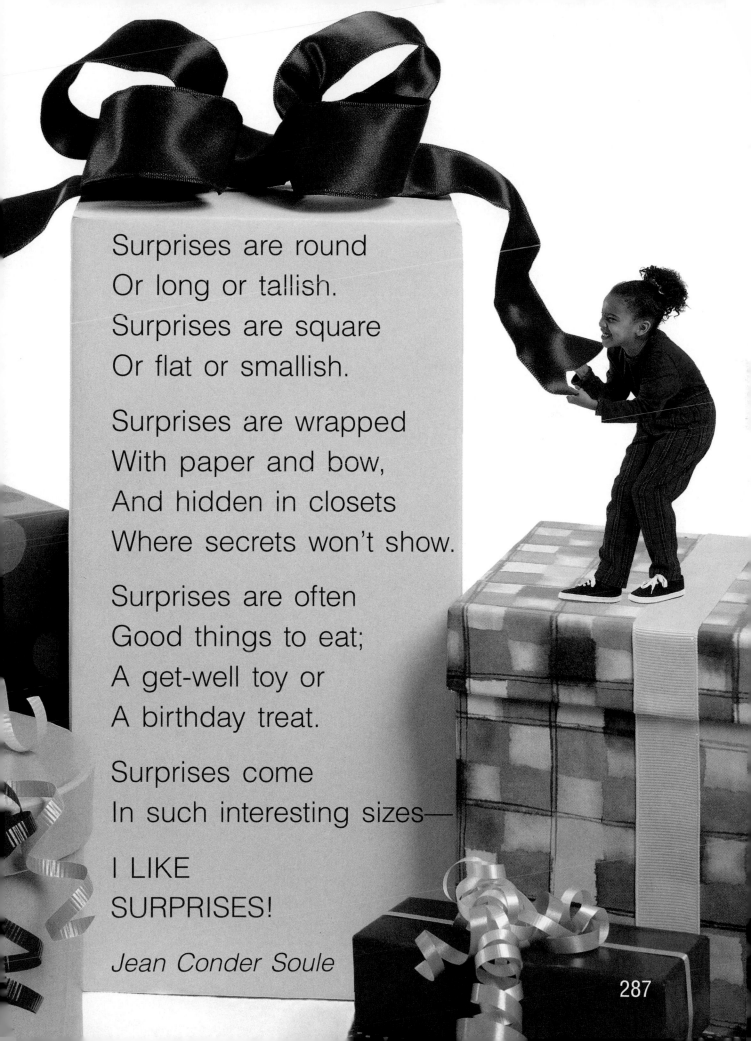

Surprises are round
Or long or tallish.
Surprises are square
Or flat or smallish.

Surprises are wrapped
With paper and bow,
And hidden in closets
Where secrets won't show.

Surprises are often
Good things to eat;
A get-well toy or
A birthday treat.

Surprises come
In such interesting sizes—

I LIKE
SURPRISES!

Jean Conder Soule

READING RESOURCES

CONTENTS

FREE PUPPIES

FREE PUPPIES

Need to find good home
for 3 puppies!
OPEN HOUSE
This Saturday afternoon
3:00 - 6:00 P.M.
3 Greenwood Lane
(corner of Main Street)
For more information call:
555-8099 after 3:00 P.M.

JACOBSON'S DEPARTMENT S

Furnitur

Men's
Clothin

Toys

Sport
Good

Jacobson's Department Store

289

BOOK PARTS

ELEPHANTS!
A Picture Book

by Marie Sandberg
Photographs by Lena Bullens

Naturebook Publications
Beaver Creek, KS

◀ **Title Page**

CONTENTS

Table of Contents ▶

CALENDAR

NOVEMBER

Sunday	Monday	Tuesday	Wednesday	Thursday	Friday	Saturday
						1
2	3	**ELECTION DAY** ✓ 4	5	6	7	8
9	10	**VETERANS DAY** 🏳 11	12	13	14	15
16	17	18	19	20	21	22
23	24	25	26	**THANKSGIVING DAY** 🍁 27	28	29
30						

Meet the Red Fox

Two Ears:
Good hearing helps the fox
when it is hunting.

Body:
Foxes have long,
soft fur that protects
them in cold weather.

Two Eyes:
The fox's eyes
are always looking
out for danger.

Nose:
The fox's
sense of
smell helps
it find food.

Four Legs:
The fox runs fast
to avoid hunters.

Tail:
The fox sleeps with its bushy tail
wrapped around its body. This
helps keep it warm and safe.

DIAGRAMS

Life in a Pond

willow tree

alder tree

dragonfly

heron

squirrel

plant life

water lilies

bullfrog

raccoon

turtles

plant life

fish

crayfish

DIRECTIONS

PAPER-PLATE MASKS

Here's what you will need:

- paper plate
- scissors
- bathroom tissue roll
- tape
- paint or markers

- glue
- construction paper, feathers, pipe cleaners, and other craft materials
- yarn

Make an Animal Mask

1.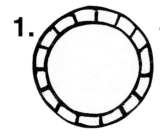
- Think of an animal mask to make.

2.
- Hold a paper plate against your face.
- Have a friend make marks for your eyes and nose.
- Then cut two eye holes and a small nose hole.

3.
- Tape the tissue roll to the plate.
- To make a beak, flatten the roll.

4.
- Trim away the bottom of the plate.

5.
- Paint or color the mask.
- Add whiskers, ears, feathers, or other items.

6.
- Poke holes at the sides of the mask.
- Pull yarn through the holes and tape down the ends.

DIRECTIONS

CHICK IN A NEST

Materials

- **cardboard egg carton**
- **scissors**
- **glue**
- **yarn, two colors**
- **construction paper**
- **paint**

Directions

1.
   - Cut one cup from the egg carton.
   - Spread glue around the outside.
   - Wind a piece of yarn around the cup.
   - Let the cup dry.

2.
   - Cut the second color of yarn into short pieces.
   - Glue them inside the cup.
   - You now have straw or twigs in a nest.

3.
   - Cut a new cup from the egg carton.
   - Turn it upside down.
   - Make sure it fits in the nest.
   - You can cut the new cup down until it does fit.

4.
   - Paint the new cup.
   - Let it dry.
   - You now have the chick's body.

5.
   - Cut the eyes and a beak from construction paper.
   - Glue them to the painted cup.
   - Then, glue the chick inside the nest.

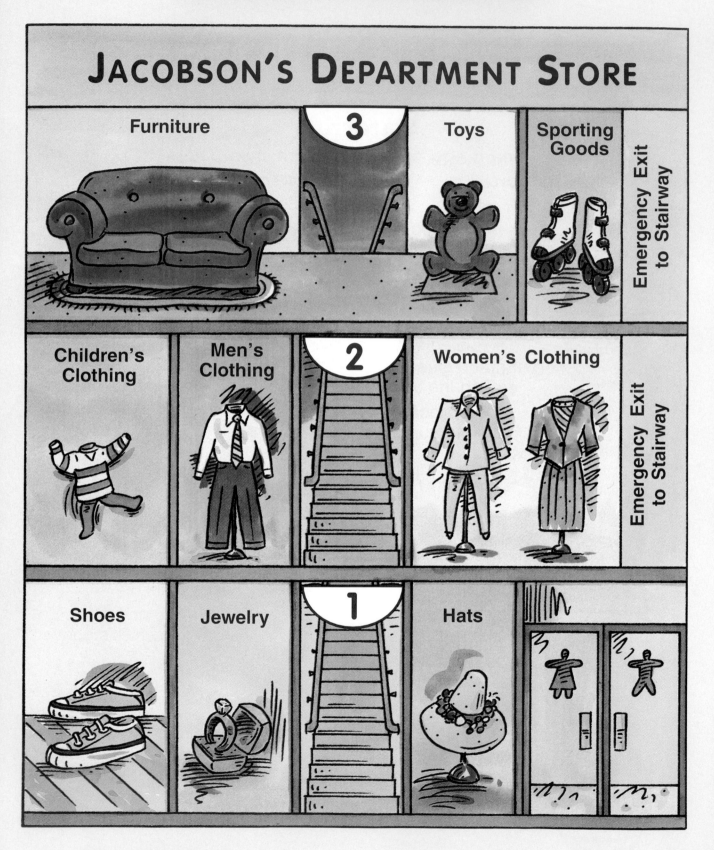

JACOBSON'S DEPARTMENT STORE

FREE PUPPIES

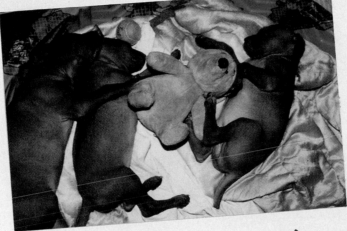

Need to find good home for 3 puppies!

OPEN HOUSE

This Saturday afternoon
3:00 - 6:00 P.M.

3 Greenwood Lane
(corner of Main Street)

For more information call:
555-8099 after 3:00 P.M.

GLOS

This glossary can help you to find out the meanings of words in this book that you may not know.

The words are listed in
alphabetical order. Guide words
at the top of each page tell you the
first and last words on the page.

Aa

across

Across means from one side to the other. Everyone ice-skated **across** the pond and then back again.

across

afternoon

Afternoon is the part of the day between noon and evening. Our school day ends at 3 o'clock in the **afternoon**. ▲ **afternoons.**

agree

When you **agree** with someone, you think or feel the same way that person does. We will **agree** to name our new cat Tabby. ▲ **agreed, agreeing.**

alligator

An **alligator** is an animal with a long body, a long tail, and short legs. It has a large mouth with many sharp teeth. **Alligators** live in rivers and swamps.
▲ **alligators.**

alligator

along

Along means together with someone or something. Do you want to come **along** with me to the park?

animal

An **animal** is anything that is alive that is not a plant and can move around by itself. A boy, a girl, a cow, a bird, a fish, and a snake are all **animals.** ▲ **animals.**

any

Any means one or some of something. You may use **any** crayon in this box.

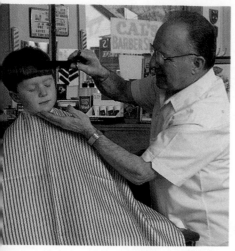
barber

Bb

barber

A **barber** is a person who cuts hair. Mom took me to the **barber** because my hair was too long. ▲ **barbers.**

beautiful

When something is **beautiful,** it is very pretty to look at or listen to. The sunset last night was **beautiful.**

body

A **body** is all of a person or an animal. An elephant has a huge, heavy **body.** ▲ **bodies.**

brother

Your **brother** is a boy who has the same mother and father as you do. My **brother** feeds the dog when he gets home from school. ▲ **brothers.**

bush

A **bush** is a plant that is smaller than a tree. A **bush** has many branches. Roses and some kinds of berries grow on **bushes**. ▲ **bushes.**

butterfly

A **butterfly** is an insect that has four large wings with bright colors. A **butterfly** landed on the flower. ▲ **butterflies.**

Cc

caterpillar

call

Call means to say something in a loud voice. Dad will **call** us when dinner is ready. ▲ **called, calling.**

caterpillar

A **caterpillar** is a baby butterfly that has a soft, long, round body, no wings, many legs, and is often furry. The **caterpillar** crawled onto her finger. ▲ **caterpillars.**

clothes

People wear **clothes** to cover their bodies. Coats, dresses, pants, and jackets are kinds of **clothes.**

cook

A **cook** is a person who makes food ready to eat. My mom is a good **cook.** ▲ **cooked, cooking.**

count

Count means to find out how many of something there are. Let's **count** how many apples we picked. ▲ **counted, counting.**

count

Dd

danger

Danger means that something could happen to hurt you. The bird escaped **danger** by flying away from the cat. ▲ **dangers.**

drink

A **drink** is a liquid you put in your mouth and swallow. Tim's favorite **drink** is milk. ▲ **drinks.**

Ee

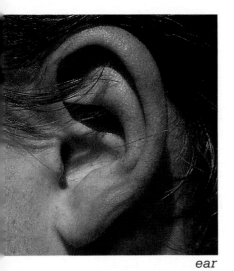

ear

ear

An **ear** is the part of the body that you hear with. There is one **ear** on each side of your head. ▲ **ears.**

elephant

An **elephant** is the biggest and strongest animal that lives on land. It has thick gray skin and a long nose called a trunk. We saw an **elephant** at the zoo. ▲ **elephants.**

everywhere

Everywhere means in all places. Betty looked **everywhere** in the house for her shoes.

G7

eye

An **eye** is the part of the body that you see with. The baby closed his **eyes** and went to sleep. ▲ **eyes.**

fall

Fall means to come down from a place. I like to watch the rain **fall** from the sky. ▲ **fell, fallen, falling.**

fall

farther

When something is **farther** away it means that it is a greater distance away. Rae's paper plane flew **farther** than Tommy's did.

food

Food is what we eat. Everything that lives needs **food** to grow. ▲ **foods.**

G g

give

Give means to let someone have something to keep. Suzy **gives** toys to her little sister. ▲ **gave, given, giving.**

great

Great means large or a lot. A **great** number of people voted in the election. ▲ **greater, greatest.**

H h

head

head

The **head** is the part of the body above the neck. Eyes, ears, nose, and mouth are all parts of the **head.** ▲ **heads.**

J j

jester

A **jester** was a person long ago who played jokes and made people laugh. The king and queen laughed at the silly **jester.** ▲ **jesters.**

K k

king

kind

Kind means a group of things that are alike in some way. Apples are a **kind** of fruit. ▲ **kinds.**

king

A **king** is a man who rules a country. I like the story about a **king** and a queen who live in a castle. ▲ **kings.**

knight

Long ago, a **knight** was a soldier for a king or queen. **Knights** wore armor and rode horses. ▲ **knights.**

knight

Ll

leg

A **leg** is a part of the body that you stand or walk on. People and animals stand and walk on their **legs.** ▲ **legs.**

Mm

morning

Morning is the part of the day before noon. I like to wake up early in the **morning** when the sun shines through my window. ▲ **mornings.**

Nn

nest

A **nest** is a bird's house. Birds build their **nests** with leaves, sticks, and mud. ▲ **nests.**

nest

nice

When something is **nice,** it makes you feel good. The sun was shining, and it was a **nice** day. ▲ **nicer, nicest.**

nose

Your **nose** is in the center of your face. You breathe and smell things through your **nose.** ▲ **noses.**

Pp

pair

A **pair** means two things that go together or something that has two legs or two parts. I need a new **pair** of socks. ▲ **pairs.**

pants

Pants are clothes that you wear on the bottom half of your body. Pants cover each leg separately. Jamie wore new **pants** to the party.

pond

A **pond** is a small lake with land all around it. The **pond** in back of my house has fish and frogs in it. ▲ **ponds.**

pond

prince

A **prince** is the son of a king or queen. Someday the **prince** will become a king. ▲ **princes.**

queen

Qq

queen

A **queen** is a woman who rules a country. The **queen** waved to the people as she rode in the carriage. ▲ **queens.**

return

Return means to come back or to go back. My cousin will **return** to France after visiting us. ▲ **returned, returning.**

S s

silly

When someone or something is **silly,** it makes us laugh. That **silly** clown did such funny things. ▲ **sillier, silliest.**

silly

sister

Your **sister** is a girl who has the same mother and father as you do. My **sister** and I both have blue eyes. ▲ **sisters.**

sock

A **sock** is a soft cover for your foot. **Socks** are worn inside shoes. ▲ **socks.**

strange

Strange means very different from what you expect. Joseph drew a picture of a **strange** animal with red ears.
▲ **stranger, strangest.**

swim

Swim means to move in the water by using arms, legs, fins, or a tail. People **swim** using their arms and legs. ▲ **swam, swum, swimming.**

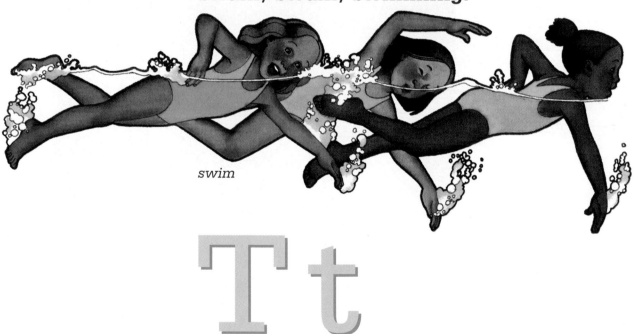

swim

Tt

tail

A **tail** is the part of an animal's body at the end of the back. Cats, dogs, and fish have **tails.** ▲ **tails.**

trouble

Trouble means that something is hard to do or might even be dangerous. Pat had **trouble** putting on his boots.
▲ **troubles.**

trunk

A **trunk** is the long nose of an elephant. Elephants use their **trunks** to pick things up. ▲ **trunks.**

trunk

turn

A **turn** is a person's time to do something. It is Dan's **turn** to hit the ball. ▲ **turns.**

G17

V v

visit

Visit means to go to see someone. Uncle Paul came to **visit** us. ▲ **visited, visiting.**

W w

water

water

Water is the liquid that falls to the ground as rain. It is in oceans, lakes, rivers, and ponds. We all need **water** to live.

waterproof

When something is **waterproof,** it will not let water go through it. Billy's raincoat was **waterproof.**